A Work of Body:
A Body of Work

poems by

Sharon Neubauer

Finishing Line Press
Georgetown, Kentucky

A Work of Body:
A Body of Work

Copyright © 2023 by Sharon Neubauer
ISBN 979-8-88838-270-7 First Edition
All rights reserved under International and Pan-American Copyright Conventions. No part of this book may be reproduced in any manner whatsoever without written permission from the publisher, except in the case of brief quotations embodied in critical articles and reviews.

ACKNOWLEDGMENTS

With deep gratitude:
To Finishing Line Press for the opportunity.
To my husband and three children who keep me living with a sense of wonder and humor.
To my ancestors, parents, and sisters whose love shaped who I am and therefore what I write.
To my friends and Yoga students who keep me exploring, questioning, looking deeper and communicating.
A special thanks to Ann Quinn and Donna Baier Stein for guidance, inspiration and encouragement.

Publisher: Leah Huete de Maines
Editor: Christen Kincaid
Cover Art: Susan Levine & Sharon Neubauer
Author Photo: Tatiana Dove
Cover Design: Susan Levine, Sharon Neubauer, & Elizabeth Maines McCleavy

Order online: www.finishinglinepress.com
also available on amazon.com

Author inquiries and mail orders:
Finishing Line Press
PO Box 1626
Georgetown, Kentucky 40324
USA

Table of Contents

Breath Body

Awakening Breath 1
Breaths 2
Breath Haiku 3
Next Breath… 4
Everyday Challenge 5

Body Parts

Cure for Sore Shoulders 9
Foot Celebration 10
Spinal Disc 11
Adjustment 12
Diaphragm 13
Chest 14
Roar 15
Mouth 16
Ear Wonder 17
Verbification 18
Body of Work 19

Mind Body

Good Morning 23
The Bind 24
Braided Thoughts 25
Before Bed 26
Selfie 27

World Body

Headstand 31
Imagination 32
Water Body 33
World Body 34

Breath Body

Awakening Breath

Breath knocks
at nostril doors
I greet my dear friend warmly
She enters cool and breezy
through tiny hairs
I show her my home

Brain office
with scattered fragments of thoughts
Tonsil sofa pillows
with memories of hard conversations
Bedroom of heart and lungs
like tear-stained blankets and hopeful images
Gut's kitchen
with command centers for fire, air, water and earth

I let Breath explore
stretch ribs to open the door more
I thank her for visiting
before bidding warm goodbye
hoping with the full weight of my soul
she will return soon

Breaths

Breath in cold, open air
offers optical reminder
of connection to breathers everywhere

Puffs waft together
creating cumulus clouds of contact
Do breaths recognize each other?

Particles of friends once joined
now separated, now merging
before splitting again

Connected
on our separate journeys
across forever

Breath Haiku

the breath is complex
yet nothing is more simple
embrace paradox

breath is nature's beat
elegant simplicity
connection to all

love is in the leaves
whistling through the air and breath
inhale to catch it

sweet inhalation
embrace connection to all
sigh in gratitude

exhale deep release
let go of what happens next
let inbreath surprise

moment's suspension
at top and bottom of breath
rest in the unknown

the pump of my life
the mobile muscle membrane
divides sky and earth

oxygenate me
over and over again
joyous mystery

Next Breath…

At the end of inbreath
there's a curlicue

a fleeting flip-turn
between receiving

and offering
a moment's savor

of gift delivered
before the hand-off

back to the infinite
a moment's choice

not to panic
at the close of outbreath

a choice to be ok
with whatever happens next

whether breath pushes off
after the flip-turn

and chooses to breeze back in
or stay out forever

Everyday Challenge

Can a full breath
be the most nourishing thing in the world

like a hot bubble bath
or a nutritious, delicious meal

let goodness sink into blood and bones
savor stretch of lungs

marvel at movements of diaphragm
envy alveoli offering oxygen to blood

such a glorious act
we get to do

over and over
over and over

from birth
to death

Body Parts

Cure for Sore Shoulders

The problem was
I dropped my heart
my shoulders ceased to carry
They let it slide
and its weary weight
sunk downward dull and dreary

My neck tried hard
to pull it up
but my arms dropped all the more
And I forgot
to let heart breathe
and shine and stretch and soar

The moon woke me
and guided my breath
with every bit of being
To reach and fill
every corner of lungs
to feel each breath as freeing

In a few short moments
I grew my heart
into my neck and shoulders
In this loving embrace
from inside out
breath became body's molder

I guided breath
into neck and collar
till it expanded my chest
And reminded me
how big I can be
and how, by breath, I'm blessed

Foot Celebration

26 bones, 29 muscles, 33 joints

infinite articulations
pleasurable pandiculations
constant cranial communications
to lowest limb gesticulations
metatarsal machinations
forming firm foot foundation
heavy home of gravitation
navicular navigation
journeying to new locations

sensitive enervation
detecting strong and light sensation
masters of adaptation
distributing weight like a substation

enormous energy emanation
squeezed into shoe immobilization
shed shoes for emancipation
let skin feel free respiration
let toes feel textured stimulation
move those toes in digitation

give them a rub when they show irritation
treat your feet with sanctification
show those toes appreciation
or bunions will grow calcification
and mess with toe configuration

feet have so much obligation
oil and rub them to keep hydration
massage them with pleasing vibration
ensuring they have strong circulation

the mind boggles at foot contemplation
Rejoice, Rejoice in foot celebration!

Spinal Disc

shock absorber for the soul
steady bone surrounds
fluid filled center
like liquid gum
boundary penetrating prevention
so gel won't go
where it doesn't belong

faces of facets
in every direction
search for information
report on position
through process procession
in parallel protrusion
providing symmetry illusion

Nature's elegant design
25 times over

Adjustment

Small pop in thoracic spine
tells of tension released

gases held tight
suddenly let   go

clearing buildup
to become   open

what do we hold
in our spaces   within

unknown airs
guarded in   gaps

stories we don't remember
swirling in cysts of invisible   spaces

within spaces
within   cells

when we let go
what fills the   void

what do we allow in
when we dare to surrender?

Diaphragm

Diaphanous diaphragm
doming upward

as I exhale
says good morning

to my happy heart
grateful for the friendship

organ to organ
drawing downward again

nudging stomach, spleen, liver
to let go of baggage

come out and play
and enjoy the ride

Chest

I rest my head
on my husband's chest
great, resonant barrel
warm skin under
combed cotton shirt
matted hair beneath
resonant voice
echoes through
chest chamber

He speaks
of uncertainty
of future, of unknown
decisions resting in others' hands
words contrast with feeling
of familiarity
of connection
certain of something
in world of uncertainty

Roar

Vocal folds
hold back sound
like a dam

divert vibration
to pool and fester

till fluctuations forge
a new path
as a stream diverts around a rock

eventually the buildup
loosens the levee and surges forth

lets loose and shares its voice
flow will find its way
and roar ahead

in a new direction
into unchartered territory

Mouth

At the orthodontist
my daughter
I want you to feel
your mouth is fine
no more this or that
contracts or contraptions

Let no man judge your smile
by faults found between gaps
in your teeth, in palate width
in stubborn newcomers
clinging to their corners
until the door is opened
just wide enough to offer place to plant

I want teeth that know their place
that see themselves as part of a whole
I want teeth that don't dominate the conversation
assuming all talk is about them
because it goes through them

And once those teeth know their place
I want jaws that know
just how much to hold back
and how much to let loose

Ear Wonder

Oh wonder that is my ear
three small bones
in three distinct shapes

small hairs
blown this way and that

by incoming vibration
bouncing off canal walls

reverberating through wind tunnel
converting to electricity

swimming through insulated wired nerves
arriving at brain which assigns meaning

mother's voice on message
shows how she worries

lowing cow in field
comforts me I have food to eat

toilet flushing in son's room
says he is home and plumbing works

passionate Beethoven
peaceful Debussy

shaping sound and balance
positioning head on spine and weight on foot

Oh wonder that is my ear,
and that I have two!
Wonder indeed!

Verbification

My shoulders have shouldered all they should shoulder
My hands handled handles offhandedly
My arms have armored and disarmed
My heart has harmed hard-heartedly

My stomach can stomach no more no less
My gut has been gut-wrenched and gutsy
I've grown a backbone and been spineless
My cheeks have been checked and cheeky

My face faced up to facts
My nose has nosed about
My mouth has mouthed off
My eyes eyed up and down

My hips have been hip and hopeless
My legs have legs to stand on
My bones have been dry and boneheaded
My knees have knee-jerk reactions

And my feet underfoot,
Have gotten cold and gotten wet
And taken a load off and been thought upon
And footed the bill for my body's debt

Body of Work

What is a body of work?

A body of work
has well-oiled hinges
repetitive motion eased by
fluids that replace on their own volition

A body of work
has well made parts that fit together
measured twice, installed once
within the millimeter

A body of work
neither squeaks nor moans
reduces friction
keeps bearings level

Or is it the exact opposite?

A body of work
slowly dries out
bearings buildup bumps
swivels swing less each year

A body of work
scars and breaks down
takes trips to the mechanic
makes do with faulty parts

Or is it both?

Every part maintained
by weight of attention
until the machine moans
and remembers its former days

Mind Body

Good Morning

Good morning cushion, supportive and waiting
Good morning highest intention, guiding my way
Good morning inadequacy, inevitable follower
Good morning insecurity, I see you're strong today
Good morning planning mind, plotting my release
Good morning escaper of moment
Good morning Creativity, already composing this poem
Good morning Ego, already planning its publication
Good morning Judger of ego; close cousin to ego
Good morning Boredom
Good morning Fear
Good morning Fear of Wasting Time
Good morning Fear of Doing it All Wrong
Good morning Fear of Never Being Seen
Good morning Need for Productivity
Good morning lasting spirits of departed grandparents
Good morning thing that is wrong with me that I can't quite express
Good morning guesser of what is wrong with me
Good morning Compassion, welcome Friend
Good morning Compassion of Judger
Good morning Compassion of Fear
Good morning Compassion of Inadequacy
Good morning hands trying to hold still
Good morning hips heavy on the earth
Good morning legs
Good morning feet awaiting instruction to walk
Good morning sitting bones settling slowly into cushioned floor
Good morning inbreath
Good morning outbreath
Good morning Breath
Good morning Meditation
Good morning Love
Now I'm ready for the day to begin

The Bind

To create a bind you press two things together
so neither can move and both are tethered.

One pushes one way, the other, the other
like opposing forces or a hug from mother.

The bind stops forward moving power
guides you to center, to contract or to flower.

The bind gives you something to push against
to discover new space or to feel condensed.

How will you feel it? The choice is yours.
Open to it or close? The possibility of doors.

Braided Thoughts

My thoughts are like ribbons
braiding around the maypole

tethered at the top and widening outward
little children on their hobby horses

threading around and through
each strand losing its foundation

till I don't know where one stops
and the other begins

But as I stand tall and see within
the nerves branching off my spine

braiding and twisting
I see through the laces

that I am the upright pole
and no matter what wraps around

my color and texture are unaltered
and the weight of the strings anchors me

I am the pole. Steady. Stable.
Unfettered. Unencumbered.

Before Bed

I let my circulation down gently
as I sit
food sloshing subsides
settles into fertile soil of sleep

If I sit long enough words will cease
I wait
while the doing
shrugs out of my body

till I hear breath
and crickets
feel feet on floor
weight lifts off brain

Here are the words
I was looking for
Good Night

Selfie

Taking a selfie
at the river
I hold the phone

this way and that
I hold my head
at one angle or another

I pull my hair to side
tie hair back
place hand to chin

hide hands from view
smile
no smile

capture river behind
frame self only
and I realize

twenty minutes have gone by
I did not note birdsong
river reflections

went unreflected upon
the nearby waterfowl family
went unnoticed

and I understand the fear
that the camera
takes away the soul

World Body

Headstand

I dig my mind
deep in earth

dendrites become
the roots of the world

gray matter
becomes soil

body becomes
stalk of soul

toes become
tree tops

and the globe
swirling around me

becomes still
Presence

Imagination

I dropped the mantras
and slogans
and intentional breaths
and simply sat on the dead log
I listened to the sounds
birds chirping
river lapping at shore
breeze blowing through branches
and riverbed

I imagined I fit in
with my rubber sole shoes
and hat knitted in distant country
I felt my bones
nestle to the log
and felt wind
move around me
like the tree trunk

and I was solid
like the earth
received air
through pores on my surface
like the soil
and I pulsed
like the water
I held heat
like the sun
harbored air and sound
like the wind
and my head opened to the heavens
and I saw myself

still

and all it took
was a little imagination

Water Body

Have I neglected you I asked the river

No you've neglected you
the river responded
for I am but a facet of you

Always moving and reflecting
showing signs of drought or abundance
at any given moment

People litter on me or nurture me
others splatter me unintentionally
I am easily drained but easily replenished

I can be easy going or sticky to mess with
I can be who I need to be
assuming the form of the banks that surround me

Bird calls surround but do not take me in
bug legs skate on me but do not delve deep
and those that delve deep never see my surface

All these are aspects of you
said the river
and I said yes, you are right

And my throat banks softened
and my mind waves washed clean
and my heart was quenched

As my watery eyes
watched the sun setting
on another day

World Body

You were dirt and you were stardust
you were ravenous predator
you were petrified prey
snatched away from mother as you snuggled
believing in love and safety
you were tasked and tired invader
missing your home far away
you were refugee
folding love letter from murdered wife
the last possession snatched before journey

You were calcium ion
forced underground in succumbing tectonic plate
birthed again to world as molehill then mountain
you were carried across the sea
found family
shaping shining shell
you were snail
nestled inside gathered safety
you were starving squid
who snatched snail from shell sanctuary

Remember all you have been
You have been predator
You have been prey
You have been provider
You have been powerless
You have been profligate and poor
poised and prone
prodigious and petite
prominent and prolapsed
Please Remember

www.ingramcontent.com/pod-product-compliance
Lightning Source LLC
Chambersburg PA
CBHW022122090426
42743CB00008B/969